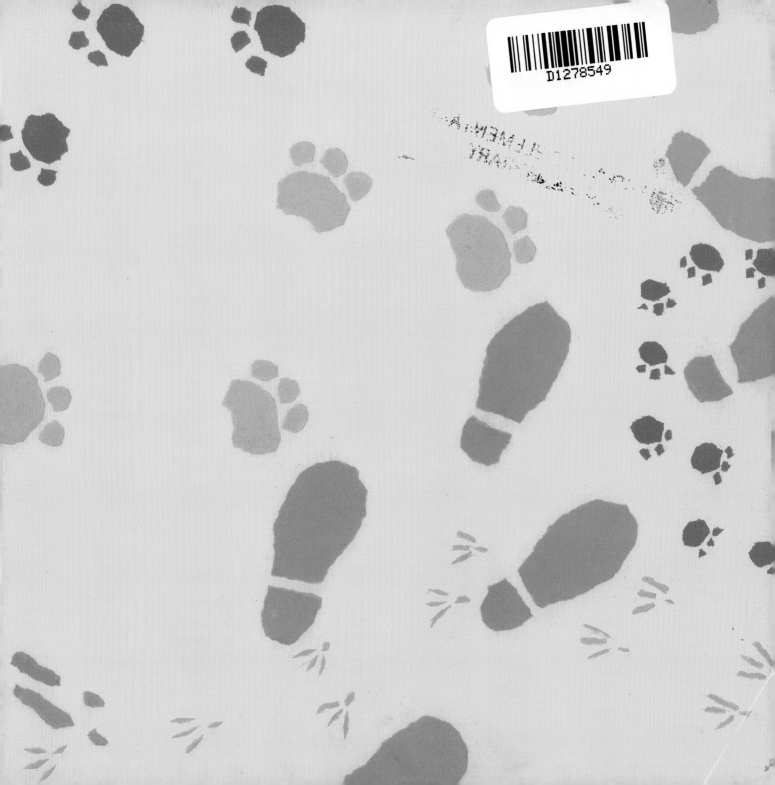

D1278549

Especially for Fuschia Singleton Hoare
and Kitty Dawkins
as they learn their first funny walks
JH

For Amelia
AA

Text copyright © 1994 Judy Hindley
Illustrations copyright © 1994 Alex Ayliffe

First published in Great Britain by ABC, All Books for Children, a division of The All Children's Company Ltd.

Published in the United States by Bridgewater Books, an imprint of Troll Associates.

All rights reserved. No part of this book may be used or reproduced in any manner whatsoever without written permission from the publisher.

Printed in Hong Kong

10 9 8 7 6 5 4 3 2 1

Library of Congress Cataloging-in-Publication Data

Hindley, Judy.
    Funny walks / by Judy Hindley ; pictures by Alex Ayliffe.
        p.   cm.
    ISBN 0-8167-3313-9 (library) — ISBN 0-8167-3314-7 (pbk.)
    1. Walking—Juvenile literature. [1. Walking.   2.   Animal
    locomotion.]   I. Ayliffe, Alex, ill.   II. Title.
    QP310.W3H56 1994
    591.1' 852—dc20   93-28446

Funny Walks

Story by Judy Hindley   Pictures by Alex Ayliffe

BridgeWater Books

Isn't it funny how
people walk?

Some of them stomp and clomp -
some of them march at a furious rate;
some of them hop and skitter and skip
and jump and race!
And dawdle and stop.

Some of them sway from leg to leg
with each of their feet
going different ways;
and some of them stride at an even pace.

Some of them bumble together in bunches
and bump and giggle and trip.

Some of them walk
with a solid step,
and a head bent down,
and a thinking face;

and some of them amble
with hands in their pockets
and faces turned up to the sky.

Oh, isn't it funny how people walk!
Do you ever walk those ways?

Isn't it odd
how animals walk,
when you take the time
to stop and watch?

Some of them trot with
   heads up high
and quick little paws lifting
   up from the ground,

scurrying this way -

scurrying that way -

stopping and dropping
their noses down,
sniffing and looking
and starting again -
trot, trot, trot -

some bounce along
on big soft paws,
and go off in a loping, gliding *run*.

Some go about
with a duck-footed waddle,
and then take a hop and a skip to get going -
pushing the ground right away from their feet -
and then they can run like a *streak!*

Have you seen one like that?

Some of them scurry
and scamper so fast,
and stop!
and creep
so s l o w . . .

And some of them hippity h o p

and then go

b o u n d i n g off with

ENORMOUS

jumps!

And some of them slink
with a velvet step,

going so soft and slow…
going so low to the ground,

or flat as a shadow against a wall (a shadow with eyes that glow).

Oh,
some little birds
(and a few big birds)
can only HOP!
from spot to spot -

hop!

hop!   hop!

And other birds stalk,
a step at a time,
one foot after
the other.

But I go about
in ALL those ways -
hopping and skipping and
    running and jumping
and bounding and bouncing
and slinking and creeping -
I shuffle and plod and
    stomp and clomp,
and march and scurry and race!

Do you want to do that, too?

Ready -

Set -

GO!

FRIENDSVILLE ELEMENTARY
SCHOOL LIBRARY